Sir Hans Sloane

by Davis LeHahn
illustrated by Cheryl Noll

HOUGHTON MIFFLIN HARCOURT
School Publishers

Printed in China

ISBN-13: 978-0-547-02168-3
ISBN-10: 0-547-02168-2

10 11 12 0940 18 17 16 15 14 13
4500443494

The Early Years

Sir Hans Sloane was a curious person. He liked to collect many things. He collected plants, animals, coins, and other souvenirs. He also collected books, insects, paintings, and rocks. He became a famous doctor, scientist, and collector. His collections grew so large that they were used to start two museums!

Sloane was born in Ireland in 1660. As a child, he was amazed by nature. He spent hours outside. He loved to study plants, and he wanted to know how plants could help sick people get better. He noticed that some people used special plants when they were sick. He wondered what other plants might help sick people become well.

In 1679, Sloane moved to London. He was still interested in science and plants. He studied chemistry and botany to learn more. He also became friends with two famous scientists. He wanted to learn as much as he could!

In 1683, he went to France to study medicine as well as botany. He continued to learn as much as he could about science. He also continued to meet many famous scientists.

Sloane was interested in many different subjects. He liked to study chemistry to learn about everything that we see, taste, touch, or feel. He also studied anatomy to learn about the parts of the body. Finally, he became a doctor. He worked as a botanist, a doctor, and a scientist, and he continued to learn new things.

A Trip to Jamaica

In 1687, Sloane sailed to Jamaica to work as a doctor. The voyage lasted three months. Sloane took many notes about what he saw during his trip. He wrote about the strange lights he saw in the water. He also wrote about the habits of sea birds that flew around the ship.

Sloane spent more than a year in Jamaica. He studied the plants that grew on the island. He took more notes on what he saw. In his notes, he explained how people used the plants. He removed some plants from the ground for his collection. He drew exact pictures of other plants in his notebook.

Sloane studied the animals that lived in Jamaica, too. He wrote about how they lived and what they ate, and even how they growled. His notes filled many books.

Sloane studied other things, too. He studied the weather, earthquakes, and rocks.

Sloane also studied the way people lived in Jamaica. He made notes about these customs in his notebook.

People in Jamaica liked a drink made from the cocoa plant. Sloane tried the drink, and at first he didn't like it. But when he added milk, he thought it tasted better. By mixing the cocoa and the milk, he created chocolate! He took his recipe for chocolate back home with him. Later, chocolate with his name on it was sold in England!

Returning to England

Sloane returned to England in 1688. He took many artifacts from Jamaica with him. He brought back books with plants pressed inside them. This kept them safe so that he could study them at home. He also brought many animals back with him.

In 1696, Sloane's notes from Jamaica were published. His book was very popular. Sloane became famous. Many important people asked him to become their doctor, including the king and queen of England.

Sloane began to collect plants and artifacts other people had discovered. His collection began to grow, and many people visited his home to see it. The halls and rooms of his house were filled with plants, animals, rocks, and coins!

Sloane bought the house next door so that he would have more room for his collection. He hired someone to guard the collection and keep it safe.

Many people tried to sell him their collections. In 1726, Benjamin Franklin traveled from America to England. He visited Sloane in London and sold him a purse.

Sloane wanted everyone to enjoy all the objects he had collected. So he asked that the objects stay together in London after his death. Sloane died in 1753 at the age of 92.

Two Museums

The government of England bought Sloane's collection. When they saw how many things he had, they realized that they had to build two museums to hold all of them.

The British Museum holds the books Sloane collected. The Natural History Museum contains his plants and other artifacts.

Today, millions of people visit these two museums. They are two of the best-known museums in the world. Sloane would be very happy to know that his work is still being shared!

British Museum

Natural History Museum

Responding

TARGET SKILL **Fact and Opinion** What facts did you learn about Sir Hans Sloane from this book? Copy this chart. On one side, write facts that you learned about Sir Hans Sloane. On the other side write your opinion about the fact.

Fact	Opinion
became a doctor ? ?	studied hard ? ?

Write About It

Text to World Sloane collected plants and artifacts from Jamaica. Write an opinion paragraph telling why it might be helpful to study things from other countries. How could this help people?

amazed	growled
discovered	guard
explained	remove
exact	souvenirs

EXPAND YOUR VOCABULARY

anatomy	chemistry
artifacts	collections
botany	customs

TARGET SKILL **Fact and Opinion** Tell if an idea can be proved or is a feeling.

TARGET STRATEGY **Question** Ask questions about what you are reading.

GENRE A **biography** tells about events in a person's life.